Dinosaurs

Parasaurolophus

by Julie Murray

1

Dash!
LEVELED READERS
An Imprint of Abdo Zoom • abdobooks.com

Dash!
LEVELED READERS

Level 1 – Beginning
Short and simple sentences with familiar words or patterns for children who are beginning to understand how letters and sounds go together.

Level 2 – Emerging
Longer words and sentences with more complex language patterns for readers who are practicing common words and letter sounds.

Level 3 – Transitional
More developed language and vocabulary for readers who are becoming more independent.

THIS BOOK CONTAINS RECYCLED MATERIALS

abdobooks.com

Published by Abdo Zoom, a division of ABDO, PO Box 398166, Minneapolis, Minnesota 55439.

Printed in the United States of America, North Mankato, Minnesota.
052024
092024

Photo Credits: Getty Images, Shutterstock
Production Contributors: Kenny Abdo, Jennie Forsberg, Grace Hansen, John Hansen
Design Contributors: Neil Klinepier

Library of Congress Control Number: 2023948545

Publisher's Cataloging in Publication Data

Names: Murray, Julie, author.
Title: Parasaurolophus / by Julie Murray
Description: Minneapolis, Minnesota : Abdo Zoom, 2025 | Series: Dinosaurs | Includes online resources and index.
Identifiers: ISBN 9781098285463 (lib. bdg.) | ISBN 9781098286163 (ebook) | ISBN 9781098286514 (Read-to-me eBook)
Subjects: LCSH: Dinosaurs--Juvenile literature. | Parasaurolophus--Juvenile literature. | Prehistoric animals--Juvenile literature. | Paleontology--Juvenile literature. | Extinct animals--Juvenile literature.
Classification: DDC 567.9--dc23

Table of Contents

Parasaurolophus

Parasaurolophus (par-ah-SAWR-ol-oh-fus) was a **hadrosaurid** dinosaur. It lived 75 million years ago.

It lived in what is now western North America.

It was more than 30 feet long (9 m). It weighed 3,000 pounds (1,360 kg).

It had four legs. It could walk on either two or four legs.

It had scales on its skin.

It had a large **crest** on its head. The crest could grow six feet (1.8 m) long!

The **crest** was used to **communicate**. It was used to make loud sounds when danger was near.

Parasaurolophus ate plants. It liked leaves, twigs, and pine needles.

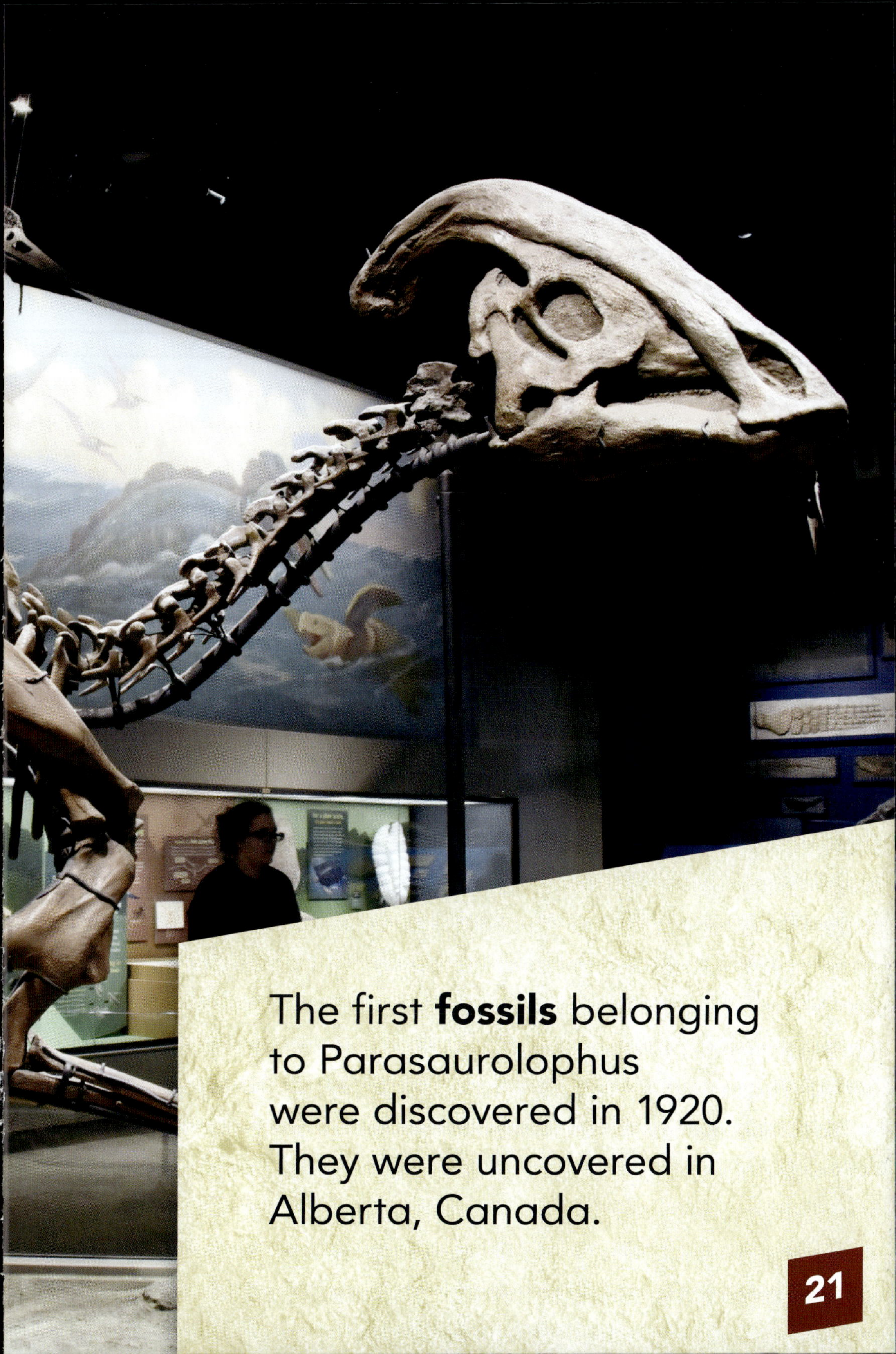

The first **fossils** belonging to Parasaurolophus were discovered in 1920. They were uncovered in Alberta, Canada.

More Facts

- *Parasaurolophus* means "near-crested lizard."
- Parasaurolophus had more than 1,000 teeth! If a tooth fell out, a new one grew.
- Its **fossils** have been found in Utah and New Mexico.

Glossary

communicate – to make known.

crest – bone on an animal's head.

fossil – the remains or trace of a living animal or plant from a long time ago. Fossils are found embedded in earth or rock.

hadrosaurid – any member of the group of dinosaurs that are also called duck-billed dinosaurs. These dinosaurs are known for the flat duck-bill appearance of the bones in their snouts.

Index

Online Resources

Booklinks
NONFICTION NETWORK
FREE! ONLINE NONFICTION RESOURCES

To learn more about Parasaurolophus, please visit **abdobooklinks.com** or scan this QR code. These links are routinely monitored and updated to provide the most current information available.